Carved wooden
bracket from a
south Indian
temple

Horse shaped
brass nutcracker

Paisley pattern
block print

Powder paints and
flowers for Holi festival

Rajasthani
puppets

Enameled
jewelry box

Mughal
frock coat

The cow is a
sacred animal
for Hindus

DK EYEWITNESS BOOKS

INDIA

Sarangi and bow

Ivory filigree
shamadaan (lantern)

Written by
MANINI CHATTERJEE and ANITA ROY

The Goddess Durga slays Mahisa,
the Buffalo Demon

DK
Dorling Kindersley

Necklace pendant
(*adiyan*) from
Gujarat

Wooden gunpowder
cask in the shape of a
mythical creature

DK

LONDON, NEW YORK, MUNICH,
MELBOURNE, and DELHI

Project editors Anita Roy, Razia Grover
Art editor Aparna Sharma
Designer Romi Chakraborty
Senior editor Carey Scott
US editors Gary Werner, Margaret Parrish
Managing art editor Clare Shedden
Picture research Kiran Mohan
Jacket design Katy Wall
Additional photography Andy Crawford
DTP designer Umesh Aggarwal

This Eyewitness ® Guide has been conceived by
Dorling Kindersley Limited and Editions Gallimard

First American Edition, 2002
03 04 05 10 9 8 7 6 5 4

Published in the United States by
DK Publishing, Inc.
375 Hudson Street
New York, New York 10014

Copyright © 2002 Dorling Kindersley Limited

19.99 / 15.57 Baker + taylor 11/05

A Cataloging-in-Publication record
is available from the Library of Congress

PLC ISBN 0-7894-8971-6
ALB ISBN 0-7894-9029-3

Bharata Natyam
dancer

Color reproduction by
Colourscan, Singapore
Printed in China by
Toppan Printing Co., (Shenzhen Ltd)

See our complete
product line at
www.dk.com

Butter churn

Baha'i House of
Worship (Delhi)

Gangaur festival
cart, Rajasthan

Contents

Wooden peacock, Tanjore, 19th century

A diverse land

Almost one fifth of all the people on earth live in India — over one billion people. They come from a huge variety of different cultures and races. From the aboriginal tribes in the tiny Andaman Islands to the mountain folk in the high Himalayas, the people of India have adapted to and settled in immensely different environments. The earliest Indians lived around 400,000 BC. Over the last 5,000 years there has been a succession of major civilizations that flourished and declined, each adding to India's fascinating history. You can find almost every type of habitat here: snowbound mountains in the north, the almost Mediterranean woodlands in the Eastern and Western Ghats (hills), deserts in Rajasthan, and lush coconut groves and tropical beaches in the south.

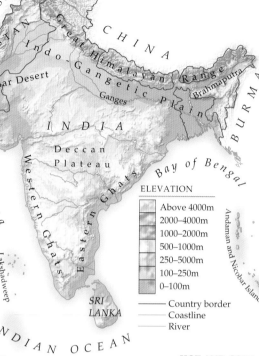

ELEVATION

	Above 4000m
	2000–4000m
	1000–2000m
	500–1000m
	250–5000m
	100–250m
	0–100m

— Country border
— Coastline
— River

DESERT NOMAD
Tribal herdsmen from Rajasthan walk miles across the dusty plains to graze their sheep and goats.

HOT AND COLD
The Indian subcontinent is a mix of many landscapes and climates. The southern tip is just 8° north of the Equator, and yet its Himalayan peaks are snowbound all year round.

PLENTY MORE FISH IN THE SEA
In Kerala, fishermen have used the same techniques for catching fish for centuries. They carve their boats from coconut tree trunks, and set sail, paddling furiously against the breaking waves. Each evening they bring in their catch to sell at the local market, and sit on the beaches mending their nets.

Coconut palms

Nets are made from nylon mesh

MILES OF SEASHORE
India is a huge peninsula, a triangle of land jutting out into the ocean. On the west is the Arabian sea, and to the east, the Bay of Bengal. The coastal communities, and the tribal peoples who live on the Andaman and Lakshadweep islands, survive by fishing. They also harvest coconuts from the groves along the shore.

THE GREAT THAR DESERT
The Thar desert in western India covers almost 70,000 sq miles (180,000 sq km). Uniquely, it has no oases nor any native varieties of cactus or palm. Temperatures here reach 122° F (50° C), but even in this inhospitable terrain humans and animals manage to live. Camels are used for transportation, and for plowing where there is enough rainfall to sustain a few hardy crops.

FROM FAR AWAY PLACES
Looks and dress vary greatly around the country. The high cheekbones and almond-shaped eyes of these Buddhist monks of the northeast are like those of Tibetans or Chinese just across the border.

Kanchenjunga peak is 28,200 ft (8,598 m) above sea level

Tea pickers collect leaves in baskets strapped to their backs

TEA PLANTATIONS
Lower mountains provide the perfect climate for tea. Famous varieties, such as Assam and Darjeeling, are named after the places where they are grown.

THE ABODE OF SNOW
The Himalayas are the world's highest mountain range. The name literally means "abode of snow," and many mountaineers have tried to scale its most famous peaks: Mount Everest, K2, and Kanchenjunga. The Himalayas form a massive natural barrier along India's northern edge, bordering China, Tibet, Nepal, and Pakistan.

The first great civilizations

Until the 1920s, the Aryan culture dating back to 1500 BC was thought to be India's oldest civilization. But in 1921, archaeologists unearthed the ruins of an entire city, buried along the banks of the Indus River in eastern India, showing that India's civilization went back much further—to 2300 BC. This city, Harappa, and another ancient city, Mohenjo-daro, now fall inside the Pakistan border. The Indus valley people who lived in these cities were as advanced as the ancient Egyptians. At about the same time as the pyramids were raised, they were constructing elaborate cities, complete with drainage systems, public baths, storehouses, granaries, and religious buildings. They traded with people from the Persian Gulf and with the Sumerians who lived in present-day Iraq.

Diadem (jeweled circlet)

Shallow grooves cut into stone for the beard

DANCING GIRL
This delicate little bronze dancing girl was found at Mohenjo-daro. Her necklace, hairstyle, and the bracelets she wears along the entire length of her arm give us a clue as to how those ancient people used to dress.

Unicorn bull engraved on a seal

INDUS VALLEY SEALS
Flat, square seals like these were probably used by merchants to stamp their goods. The strange symbols at the top are a very early form of writing. Thousands of these baked soapstone tablets have been found.

Two deer fighting with locked antlers

Amulet worn high up on the arm

HAIR CARE
A vast number of ornate hairpins have been found among the remains of the Indus valley settlements. Copper hairpins, like this one, would have been used by Harappan women to fix their long hair in place.

THE BEARDED MAN
This famous sculpture was found in a small house in the lower city of Mohenjo-daro. The diadem on his head, his ceremonial robe, and his serene expression suggest that he may have been a head priest or a Harappan god. Clay figurines of mother-goddesses have also been found, indicating that Harappans practiced idol worship—revering statues as gods.

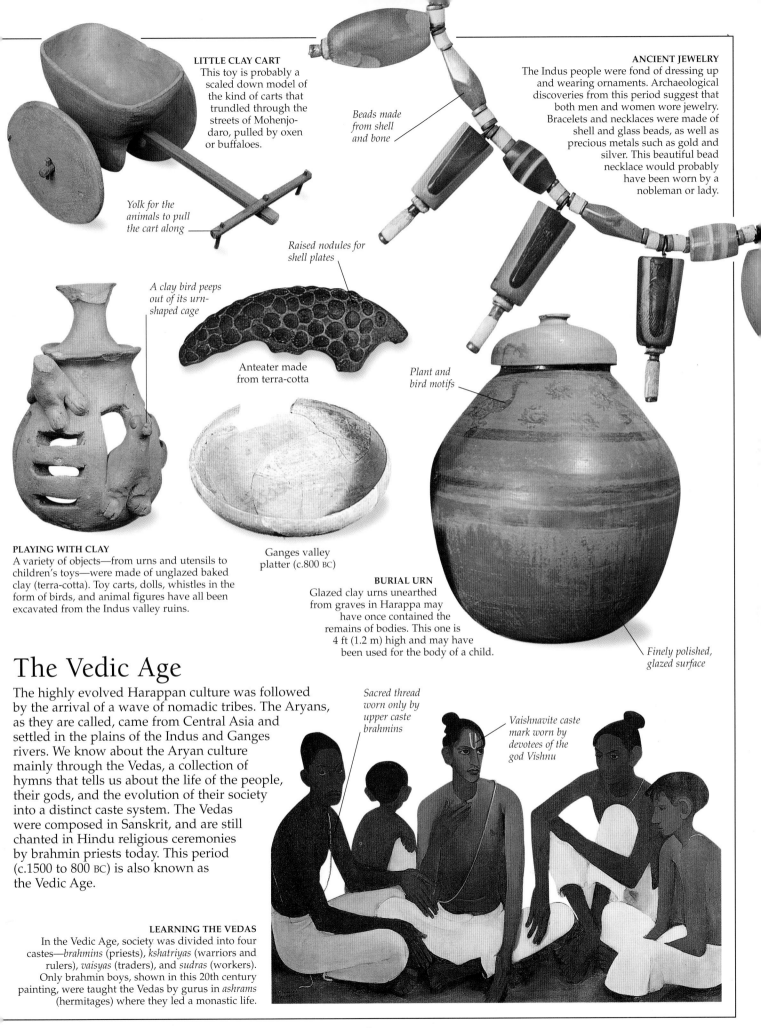

LITTLE CLAY CART
This toy is probably a scaled down model of the kind of carts that trundled through the streets of Mohenjo-daro, pulled by oxen or buffaloes.

Yolk for the animals to pull the cart along

ANCIENT JEWELRY
The Indus people were fond of dressing up and wearing ornaments. Archaeological discoveries from this period suggest that both men and women wore jewelry. Bracelets and necklaces were made of shell and glass beads, as well as precious metals such as gold and silver. This beautiful bead necklace would probably have been worn by a nobleman or lady.

Beads made from shell and bone

Raised nodules for shell plates

A clay bird peeps out of its urn-shaped cage

Anteater made from terra-cotta

Plant and bird motifs

PLAYING WITH CLAY
A variety of objects—from urns and utensils to children's toys—were made of unglazed baked clay (terra-cotta). Toy carts, dolls, whistles in the form of birds, and animal figures have all been excavated from the Indus valley ruins.

Ganges valley platter (c.800 BC)

BURIAL URN
Glazed clay urns unearthed from graves in Harappa may have once contained the remains of bodies. This one is 4 ft (1.2 m) high and may have been used for the body of a child.

Finely polished, glazed surface

The Vedic Age
The highly evolved Harappan culture was followed by the arrival of a wave of nomadic tribes. The Aryans, as they are called, came from Central Asia and settled in the plains of the Indus and Ganges rivers. We know about the Aryan culture mainly through the Vedas, a collection of hymns that tells us about the life of the people, their gods, and the evolution of their society into a distinct caste system. The Vedas were composed in Sanskrit, and are still chanted in Hindu religious ceremonies by brahmin priests today. This period (c.1500 to 800 BC) is also known as the Vedic Age.

Sacred thread worn only by upper caste brahmins

Vaishnavite caste mark worn by devotees of the god Vishnu

LEARNING THE VEDAS
In the Vedic Age, society was divided into four castes—*brahmins* (priests), *kshatriyas* (warriors and rulers), *vaisyas* (traders), and *sudras* (workers). Only brahmin boys, shown in this 20th century painting, were taught the Vedas by gurus in *ashrams* (hermitages) where they led a monastic life.

The land of the Buddha

THE PASTORAL LIFESTYLE of the Vedic age slowly gave way to settled farming and the beginnings of towns and cities. This new era saw the rise of two remarkable preachers, both from noble families, who gave up their posessions to lead lives of spiritualism and simplicity. One was a prince of the Sakya clan called Siddhartha Gautama who left his home and wandered for six years, finally achieving *nirvana* (enlightenment). He became known as the Buddha, or "Enlightened One." The other was Vardhamana, who was similarly renamed Mahavira ("great hero") and whose followers were known as Jains. Both Buddhists and Jains rejected the rigid caste system of the Aryan Hindus. This, and their belief in nonviolence and social equality, gained them many followers.

SACRED SITE
The most sacred Buddhist site in India is this large stupa (burial mound) at Sanchi, in central India. It was built in the 3rd century BC by the great emperor Ashoka, who ruled his empire according to Buddhist principles.

Prince Siddhartha gives up his horse and groom

Prince Siddhartha leaves his harem

THE GREAT DEPARTURE
This is a section of a large frieze from the Amaravati stupa in south India. It shows Prince Siddhartha leaving his luxurious palace for an austere life in search of spiritual truth and an end to human suffering.

Prince Siddhartha secretly leaves his palace on his horse Kanthaka

Sleeping woman

Cells where monks would go into retreat

Robes worn by Buddhist monks are usually yellow and orange, the colors of the rising sun

LEARN AND TEACH
Many families made sure that their eldest son joined a monastery. Here he would be looked after and taught by monks, and would learn all about the Buddhist way of life.

CENTER OF LEARNING
One of the oldest universities in the world, Nalanda, in eastern India, dates back to the 5th century AD. It was built on a pilgrimage site visited by Buddha. Monasteries set up by his followers throughout the country became important centers of learning, culture, and art.

A vast mound covered the site before it was discovered in the late 1800s

THE ENLIGHTENED ONE

After 49 days of meditation under a tree at a place that came to be known as Bodh Gaya, Siddhartha attained enlightenment. After this, he was called Buddha, which means "the Enlightened One." He spent the remaining 44 years of his long life wandering from place to place and teaching that suffering is caused by desire, and that only by ending desire can one put an end to suffering. Desire could be conquered by following the "Eightfold Path" of right thought, action, effort, understanding, speech, livelihood, concentration, and contemplation. This golden statue of Buddha meditating was a gift to the Indian people from the spiritual leader of Tibet, the Dalai Lama.

Words of the mantra inscribed on brass

Weighted chain helps the wheel to spin

A mantra (prayer) is written down and rolled up inside

Lower lid

Wooden grip is spun around

SIMPLE SEEKERS

Buddhism remained very popular in India for several centuries after Buddha's death because it rejected the costly rituals and caste system practiced by Hindu priests. Buddhist monks were simple seekers, who went from door to door with begging bowls for people to fill with food.

PRAYER WHEEL

Buddhists believe that they gain spiritual merit with each prayer recited. Instead of chanting it out loud, every turn of the special prayer wheel counts as a prayer uttered.

Right hand turned down, asking the earth to witness his enlightenment

Lotus flower pedestal on which Buddha is usually shown seated or standing

Two ancient empires

KINGDOMS ROSE AND FELL, but two great empires of ancient India – the Mauryas and the Guptas – have left a lasting legacy. The Mauryan empire (322–185 BC) began with Chandragupta Maurya, a warrior king. He extended his empire from the east to the northwest, after defeating one of Alexander the Great's generals. Chandragupta's grandson, Ashoka, became the greatest Maurya ruler of all. Ashoka was strongly influenced by Buddhist ideals. He had edicts (rules), instructing his subjects in the importance of nonviolence and correct ethical behavior, inscribed on stone pillars throughout the country. The Maurya empire then broke up into smaller kingdoms until the 4th century AD, when the Hindu king, Chandragupta I, established the Gupta empire, a "Golden Age" that lasted more than 200 years.

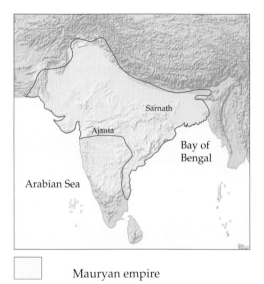

Mauryan empire

Gupta empire

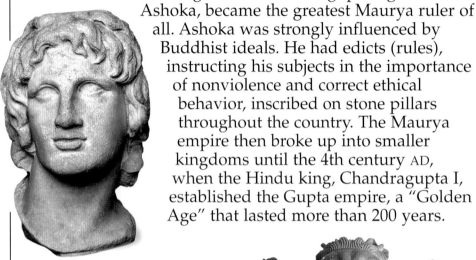

ALEXANDER THE GREAT
Ruler of one of the largest empires in the world, the Greek king Alexander marched into Punjab in north India in 326 BC. After his death three years later, his generals were defeated by Chandragupta Maurya.

Letters carved on the rock surface

WRITTEN IN STONE
Ashoka's edicts were mainly written in Pali, a language that was more accessible to common people than Sanskrit. He appointed officials to make sure these Buddhist "rules of conduct" (*dhamma*) were followed.

The 24-spoked chakra (wheel) symbolizes the Buddhist Wheel of Law

ASHOKAN CAPITAL
Some of Ashoka's edicts were also carved on polished sandstone pillars, usually topped with animal "capitals." The lion capital from Sarnath in north India was adopted as India's official emblem, and can be found on all modern coins and currency notes.

GANDHARA SCULPTURE
These 1st century AD carvings of Buddha, from the northwestern province of Gandhara, display traces of classical Greek art. This was due to the influence of the descendants of Alexander's generals who settled there.

Greek features like coiled hair are typical of Gandhara art

The emperor playing music

Gold coins of Samudragupta

WEALTH OF THE GUPTAS
Chandragupta I, Samudragupta, and Chandragupta II, the three great kings of the Gupta dynasty, were generous patrons of learning and culture. Their gold coins reflect an age of prosperity.

Elongated ear lobes also found on Buddhist statues

HINDU HOLY TRINITY
The Gupta era was called a "Golden Age" as much for its artistic wealth as its economic prosperity. This stone carving from the period shows the three main gods in the Hindu religion: Brahma (the creator), Vishnu (the preserver), and Shiva (the destroyer).

Ceiling vaults carved from solid rock

CAVE TEMPLES
Prayer halls with high vaulted ceilings and carved beams are a typical feature of the Buddhist cave temples of Ajanta and Ellora.

AJANTA FRESCO
The 2nd century BC cave monastery at Ajanta in central India is famous for its frescoes (wall paintings). These tell the story of Buddha's life and past incarnations. The artists who painted them were funded by royal patrons. They coated the cave walls with mud and lime to make a base, and used natural minerals, such as yellow and orange ocher, for the paintings. The image on the left is a detail from a court scene. Forgotten for more than a thousand years, the frescoes were rediscovered in the 19th century.

Conflicts in the north

FOR MORE THAN A THOUSAND years, from the end of the Gupta empire to the coming of the Mughals (pp.18–19), no single dynasty was able to establish an empire in the subcontinent. North India remained in a state of turmoil with different factions competing for power. The final blow to the Gupta dynasty was dealt by the Huns, a military tribe from central Asia, who repeatedly invaded from the northwest and established their rule at the end of the 5th century AD. They did not rule for long and were displaced by a succession of rulers. The only memorable king of that time is Harshavardhana (AD 606-647), who conquered many parts of north and east India. For the next four centuries, a handful of local kingdoms battled for supremacy, with no clear winner. Taking advantage of this, the Turkish warlord, Mohammad Ghori, defeated the Rajput king of Delhi, Prithviraj Chauhan, in 1192. Ghori's general, Qutbuddin Aibak, established the first of many Muslim dynasties, which reached their height with the great Mughals over three hundred years later.

Sharp ax blade

Spiked mace to pierce armor

Handle unscrews to reveal sword inside

SELF DEFENSE
The knuckleduster was a simple but powerful weapon for hand-to-hand combat. This one is made of buffalo horn.

Rajput warrior being attacked by a lion

An archer stringing his bow

Curved metal nodules to deflect arrows and blades

Battle-ax from the Deccan region in central India

INSTRUMENTS OF WAR
The weapon-makers of ancient India created lethal but beautiful weapons of war. Maces, battle-axes, and swords were made so skillfully that they could actually break through helmets and smash thick plates of armor.

RAJPUT SHIELD
Rajput clans claimed warrior (*kshatriya*) status. They were a courageous race whose exploits are recorded in history books and were sung about by village bards. Although they fought the Mughals, the Rajputs also made many military alliances with them and even married into Mughal families. They were also strongly influenced by the Mughals' fine artistic sense, as reflected in this beautiful shield.

Sliding nasal bar protected the nose

Chainmail protected the neck and shoulders

RAMPARTS AND BASTIONS

With the entry of Turk, Arab, and Afghan adventurers into north India in the 12th century, the fort became an important building for defense. The fort at Jaisalmer was one of the most strategically important, since it lay on the trade route from Persia into India. The Sultan of Delhi, Alauddin Khilji, accused Jaisalmer's Rajput *rawal* (chieftain) of having plundered his caravan of precious goods, and he laid siege to the fort for eight long years. Finally, in 1295, the Rajput forces were defeated in a tremendous battle in which 24,000 women and children living inside the fortress walls were killed.

HEAD PROTECTION

Indian kings had huge armies of foot soldiers who wore armor such as the engraved helmet shown above. The skillfully worked chainmail provided much needed protection against enemy arrows and swords. But foot soldiers in the best armor in the world could not defeat invaders mounted on swift, sturdy horses.

THE COMING OF ISLAM

The five-story Qutb (pole or axis) Minar (tower) in Delhi was begun in 1193 by Qutbuddin Aibak, a slave who rose to become a general, and finally the ruler of the Mamluk (Slave) dynasty (AD 1206–46). This massive stone structure was, for many years, the world's highest single tower. The *minar* marked Aibak's victory over the Rajputs, and the start of Muslim rule in India. It took stonemasons and sculptors over 150 years to build, and was finally completed in 1368.

Verses from the Qur'an engraved in stone

Quwwat-ul-Islam "Might of Islam" mosque

Kingdoms of the south

WHILE CONFLICTS RAGED in the north, the southern kingdoms flourished. During the 5th century AD, the powerful Pallava dynasty developed strong trade links with southeast Asia from its capital, Kanchipuram. But it was the Cholas who, in the 9th century, gained control of most of the south, defeating the Pallavas. The Chola kings were great patrons of the arts, and many fine bronze temple sculptures date to this time. Their great wealth came from selling silks, spices, and gems to Egypt and Rome, as well as Arabia, China, and southeast Asia. In 1216, the Cholas were defeated by the Pandyas who ruled until the early 14th century. They were succeeded in turn by the Vijayanagar empire, which dominated until 1565.

Elaborate headdress

Hundreds of Hindu gods are sculpted and painted on the towering façade

CHOLA BRONZES
The Cholas were one of the most powerful dynasties of the south. They were devout Hindus and were famous for their beautiful bronze figurines, such as this one of the goddess Parvati, wife of Lord Shiva. The bronzes were kept inside the shrine while the outer walls were decorated with elaborately carved stone friezes.

Graceful line from fingertip to shoulder

A pillar of strength, the monkey god Hanuman is said to have carried a whole mountain back to Lord Ram

The pointed "temple" motif is common to many south Indian saris

KANCHIPURAM SILK

As the capital city of the Pallava empire, Kanchipuram was a vibrant trading city and the silk capital of India. It gave its name to the sumptuous silks created by its master weavers. The silk was often interwoven with threads of pure gold to give a special sheen. Although the town lost its status with the fall of the Pallava dynasty in the 9th century AD, it still produces the country's finest silk saris today.

THE AGE OF GOLD

Along with silk, spices, and sandalwood, gold played an important part in the wealth of southern India. At their height, the Chola kings controlled not only every important trading center in the South, but also the gold mines and pearl fisheries of Ceylon (present-day Sri Lanka). This wealth was used to fund their armies, as well as to make rich ornaments for themselves and their wives.

Intricate gold filigree

Lakshmi, the goddess of wealth

Large rubies

Buddha seated on a lotus

FRAGRANT WOOD

Traders in the south grew rich by harvesting and exporting sandalwood, which was prized for its heavenly scent.

SPICE AND FRAGRANCE

Spices from south India were highly prized throughout the world. Cardamoms, cinnamon, and cloves grew in abundance and were shipped to Europe. In 17th century England, peppercorns from south India were worth their weight in silver!

Black peppercorns

Cloves

Cardamom pods

GATEWAY TO HEAVEN

The crowning glory of south Indian temples is the *gopuram* — a profusely carved gateway soaring toward the sky. The four *gopurams* of the splendid Meenakshi temple in Madurai are considered the most magnificent. The temple complex was begun by the Vijayanagar rulers in the 15th century AD. Each successive ruler and their queens added to the temple, so that eventually each temple had many structures and *gopurams*.

The many-armed goddess Durga slays the buffalo-demon, lying at her feet

A many-headed cobra spreads its hood

The god Vishnu as "Narasimha" half-man, half-lion

HAMPI NARASIMHA

The Vijayanagara empire collapsed after a great battle in January 1565, when king Ramaraya's army was defeated by the combined forces of various sultans. Vijayanagar literally means "City of Victory," but after this defeat, the capital, at Hampi, fell into ruins. Most of the temples were destroyed but some stone statues, such as this Narasimha, carved from a single boulder in 1528, still survive.

The great Mughals

Talisman (*tabeez*) with verses from the Koran

THE MUGHALS WERE ONE of the world's great medieval dynasties (empires). Babur was the first Mughal ruler. He invaded from the plains of central Asia in AD 1526, and his descendants then ruled for over 200 years. By the end of the 17th century, the empire covered almost the entire country, apart from the extreme southern tip. The Mughals brought many new ideas with them—in architecture, warfare, and the arts—but their most important contribution was perhaps the introduction of Islam to the country. Many of India's best known monuments, such as the Taj Mahal, are Islamic structures built by the Mughals. When the last great emperor, Aurangzeb, died in 1707, the empire declined and it was soon replaced by British rule.

Brass breast-plates protect upper body

A solitary pearl hangs from the tip

Tobacco is stored in the upper casket

Center stone is a large ruby

MUGHAL JEWELS
The Mughals had a passion for jewelry, especially precious stones. Diamonds, emeralds, rubies, sapphires, and pearls were used extensively in ornaments such as this *sarpech*, a jeweled brooch worn on royal turbans. Emperors Jahangir and Shah Jahan were said to possess the most fabulous collection of jewels on earth.

HUBBLE BUBBLE
Smoking a hookah pipe was a pleasurable pastime among royalty and commoners. This elaborate silver hookah, crafted in the shape of a peahen and her chick, may have been used by the ladies in the emperor's harem.

RESPLENDENT ROBES
In keeping with their love of splendor, Mughal costumes were made of brocade and silk, richly woven or embroidered with gold and silver thread, known as *zari*, and encrusted with precious stones.

BABUR
Babur descended on his father's side from the 14th-century Turkish warlord, Timur (Tamburlaine), and on his mother's side from Chengiz (Ghenghis) Khan, the fearsome Mongol chieftain. Although he was a fiery warrior, he was also a great nature lover. Babur ruled for four years until his death in 1530. The *Baburnama* gives a vivid account of his life and times.

1526–30

HUMAYUN
Babur's son Humayun had two separate periods of rule. He was deposed in 1540 by the Afghan chieftain Sher Shah Suri, and then spent many years in wars against his brothers beyond India's northwest frontier. In 1555, he regained Delhi after defeating Sher Shah's successors. Humayun died in a tragic accident in 1556 when he tripped down the steep stairs of his library.

1530–40, 1555–56

AKBAR
Akbar was only 13 when his father died. The young king extended the empire through conquests and alliances with Hindu kings. He tried to establish a new religion blending Islam and Hinduism. He established an extensive civil service to run the empire, created a magnificent library in his capital near Agra, and encouraged music, wit, and lively debates in his court.

1556–1605

The hilt of this 17th-century sword is shaped like a ram's head

Gold inlay

Both sides of the dagger are razor-sharp

SWORDS OF EMPIRE
Mughal armorers were highly skilled in casting metal. Swords were often decorated with jewels, silver leaf, and gilt. Even ceremonial swords like these were kept extremely sharp.

Golden goblet engraved with dancing girls, deers, and flowers

WINING AND DINING
Travelers to Mughal India wrote of the lavish feasts that took place in the court. One such writer described a meal where he was presented with no less than 50 different dishes to choose from, all on silver and gold platters. The emperor would sip wine from an enameled silver or gold goblet. He would be served by royal eunuchs.

HUMAYUN'S TOMB
Humayun's tomb in Delhi was the first grand tomb of the Mughal period. It was built by Humayun's widow, Haji Begum, and finished in 1573. The elegant proportions of the building and surrounding gardens, and the white marble dome, are thought to have inspired the design of the Taj Mahal.

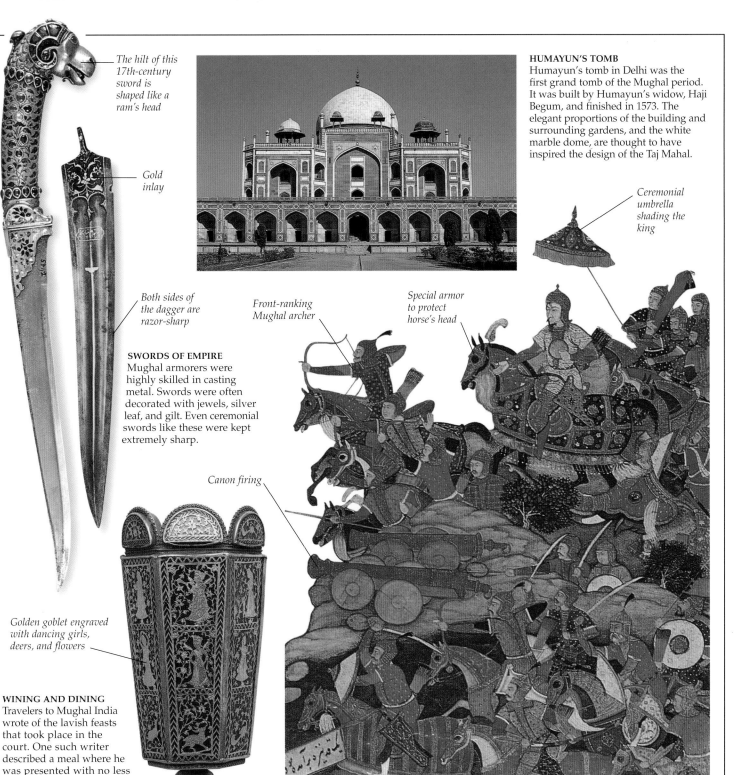

Ceremonial umbrella shading the king

Front-ranking Mughal archer

Special armor to protect horse's head

Canon firing

THE FIRST BATTLE OF PANIPAT
This miniature painting is an illustration from the *Baburnama*—the biography of the first Mughal king, Babur. It shows a scene from the Battle of Panipat which took place in April 1526 between Babur and the Sultan of Delhi, Ibrahim Lodi. It was the first time that guns and muskets were used in northern India, which helped the Mughals to win.

JAHANGIR
Jahangir inherited a stable empire, allowing him to pursue his interest in the arts, which flourished under his patronage. His wife, Noor Jahan, wielded great power from the harem. Jahangir was a nature lover and designed beautiful gardens. He kept a detailed diary, and his reign is also described in the account left by Sir Thomas Roe, Britain's first ambassador to India.

1605–27

SHAH JAHAN
Under Shah Jahan, the Mughal empire reached its height of pomp and grandeur, reflected in Shah Jahan's passion for architecture. He designed the Taj Mahal in memory of his beloved wife, Mumtaz Mahal, and also built a splendid capital, Shahjahanabad, in Delhi. Dethroned by his son, he spent his last days in captivity at Agra Fort, gazing wistfully toward the Taj.

1627–58

AURANGZEB
Aurangzeb, the last great Mughal, ruthlessly killed his brothers and exiled his father in order to ascend the throne. Unlike his forefathers, he was austere and orthodox, and tried to impose a strict Islamic regime. This led to many revolts, forcing Aurangzeb into costly wars. He expanded the empire but it went bankrupt, and began to disintegrate soon after his death.

1658–1707

The Taj Mahal

THE MAGNIFICENT TAJ MAHAL has long been known as the "eighth wonder of the world." It was built in the 17th century by the Mughal emperor Shah Jahan as a memorial to his beloved wife Mumtaz Mahal. It took about 20,000 people almost 22 years to build, and its construction was personally overseen by the emperor himself. Taj Mahal literally means the "crown of palaces," and no less than 43 varieties of precious and semiprecious stones make up the jewels in this crown. This garden tomb is renowned for its perfect symmetry: it is exactly as wide as it is high, and the dome is exactly the same height as its arched façade. In its lavish use of expensive materials, perfectly balanced proportions, and its intricate decorations, the Taj symbolizes the wealth of the Mughal empire, and the refined taste of its rulers.

MUMTAZ MAHAL
Arjumand Banu Begum (1593–1631), Shah Jahan's favorite wife, was given the title Mumtaz Mahal, which means the "chosen one of the palace."

PLAYING WITH PERSPECTIVE
Verses from the Koran, the holy book of Islam, are picked out in black stone all around the main arch. The letters at the top are bigger, so for anyone looking up, they appear to be the same size!

PIETRA DURA
The art of inlaying slivers of colored stone into marble is called *pietra dura*, which literally means "hard stone" in Italian. A single bloom on the tomb of Mumtaz Mahal is said to contain 35 different precious stones.

Each of the four corner minarets is 131 ft (40 m) high. They emphasize the perfect symmetry of the complex

Carnelians from Baghdad and amethysts from Persia were among the stones used for the flawless pietra dura *work*

The outer marble dome rises high above a central inner one

Eight-sided trellis of white marble encloses the tombs

ROYAL TOMB CHAMBER
Mumtaz Mahal and Shah Jahan's tombs stand on a raised platform in the exact center of the monument. The actual graves, in a dark crypt below, are closed to the public. Mumtaz Mahal died in childbirth while she was accompanying Shah Jahan on one of his military campaigns. The emperor was so stricken by grief that it is said his hair turned completely white. He planned to build an exact replica of the Taj in black marble on the opposite bank of the river as his final resting place, but this was never built, so he was buried next to his beloved wife.

The minarets are crowned by a chhatri (canopy), which was used for the azan *(call to prayer)*

ARCH AND TRELLIS
Perforated screens were intricately carved from single blocks of marble. Like the lacy veils worn by Muslim women, these patterned trellises allow you to see out, but no one else to see in.

Cypress trees line the central canal

THE PARADISE GARDEN
Mughal formal gardens were called *charbaghs* (four gardens). The four quarters were divided by raised walkways, sunken groves, and water channels. The Taj is situated at one end of the *charbagh*, unlike most garden tombs which were in the middle. The *charbagh* was thought to be a replica of the garden of paradise.

Arrival of the Europeans

SINCE THE 14TH CENTURY, Indian silks and spices had been brought into Europe by Arab merchants. But when the Turks captured Constantinople in 1453, blocking this overland trade route, Europe was forced to look for other routes to the East. Christopher Columbus set out on this quest, but took a wrong turn and "discovered" America instead. The Portuguese seafarer Vasco da Gama was luckier and arrived on the shores of India in 1498, closely followed by the English, Dutch, and French. The Dutch and English East India Companies were set up in the early 1600s to supply textiles and spices to the growing European market. India was seen as a source of huge potential wealth, and was fiercely fought over. Robert Clive, who defeated the Nawab of Bengal at the Battle of Plassey in 1757, was one of the first to realize that, with sufficient military force, Britain could vastly increase its wealth by making India not a trading partner, but a colony.

RIDING HIGH
Like the maharajas before them, European traders and conquerors traveled in style on the backs of richly decorated elephants, led by their mahouts.

TRADERS FROM HOLLAND
The Dutch East India Company was set up in 1602 to carry textiles and spices from Indonesia and India. This wooden doll is of a Dutch naval officer whose job was to oversee the loading and unloading of a ship's precious cargo.

ROBERT CLIVE
From humble beginnings as an East India Company clerk in Madras, Clive became one of the richest and most powerful men in the country. He was a great military leader and won many battles.

"The inhabitants [of Bengal] are servile, mean, submissive, and humble. In superior stations, they are luxurious, effeminate, tyrannical, treacherous, venal, cruel. The country ... abounds in very curious and valuable manufactures, sufficient not only for its own use, but for the use of the whole globe."

ROBERT CLIVE
Colonel and Governor of Bengal, 1772

பஜார் செயின்டலொரான் வீதி
RUE DU BAZAR SAINT LAURENT

THE FRENCH IN INDIA
This signpost in Pondicherry, on India's southeastern coast, is written in Tamil and French. Both languages are still spoken in the 16th-century town, which the French developed into a port and administrative center.

Calicut

Route of Vasco da Gama's expedition

Long musket-barrel

JOSEPH FRANÇOIS DUPLEIX
This brilliant statesman wanted to establish French supremacy in south India. He became governor of Pondicherry in 1742.

Gunpowder was kept in a ram's horn keg

PORTUGUESE VOYAGER
Vasco da Gama was the first European to sail to India. The expedition took 10 months to sail from Lisbon, Portugal, to Calicut on India's southwest coast. Da Gama died soon after he was appointed Portuguese viceroy to India in 1524.

LOYAL FOOT SOLDIERS
Many Indians served in the British army as private soldiers. The British called these foot soldiers "sepoys."

FORT ST. GEORGE, MADRAS
In 1639, the British East India Company founded the port of Fort St. George. This city, on the southwest coast, was later renamed Madras, and is now called Chennai. This engraving shows the ships lining up outside the harbor. Goods, such as silks and spices, were loaded into small rowing boats and taken to where the ships were anchored. Although the European trading ships were small by today's standards, they had surprisingly large holds to carry back their hauls from India. Provisions such as dried meat, fruit, and fresh water were also taken on board for the crew's long journey back to Europe. The other main ports at this time were Surat, on the west coast, and Calcutta (now Kolkata) in the east.

The British Raj

IMPERIAL HAT TRICK
The sola topi was such a common sight during Britain's rule, that it came to symbolize the Raj.

DURING THE 100 YEARS following Robert Clive's victory at Plassey (see p. 22), the British extended their control over India on every front: economic, political, military, and social. They quelled local uprisings, the most important being the "mutiny" of 1857 when Indian troops took up arms against their British masters. The British Raj was established a year later, as the country was finally brought under full imperial rule by Queen Victoria and was governed from London. The 19th century industrial revolution thrived by importing cheap, raw materials from India, and selling expensive, manufactured products back to the colony. The Raj drained India's wealth, and denied political rights to its people, but it also politically united the country, constructed railroads, and set up a centralized administrative and judicial system.

VICTORIA REGINA
Queen Victoria was more attached to India than to any other part of the British Empire. On January 1, 1877, a grand Durbar ceremony was held in Delhi to proclaim Queen Victoria *Kaiser-i-Hind*, Queen-Empress of India. India's governor general became the Queen's viceroy and chief representative in India.

TIPU'S TIGER
Hunting tigers was a popular sport for the British in India, as it was for the Maharajas before them. This Victorian model is actually a toy organ. The tiger devouring a hapless British soldier is said to represent Tipu, the ruler of Mysore, who had defeated the British in the 18th century.

Openings at the top of the organ pipes

Insignia of one of the Indian railway lines

Organ keys in the tiger's tummy

MAKING TRACKS
The British laid a vast network of railroads across the length and breadth of the country. The first steam locomotive set off from Bombay in 1853. By 1880, over 9,000 miles (14,400 km) of track had been laid. Engineers even cut through steep mountain slopes to reach the hill stations, such as Shimla.

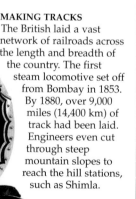

HUNTLEY & PALMERS
BISCUITS

A TASTE OF ENGLAND
The very English institution of "high tea" became part of daily life for many well-to-do Indians during the Raj. This early 20th-century cookie tin shows everyone from maharajas to army generals lining up to sample their favorite cookies.

SUMMER CAPITAL

Every summer, almost the entire British population of Delhi would move to the cooler climes of Shimla. Known as "the Queen of the Hills," Shimla became the summer capital for the Raj. Grand balls for over 800 people were held at the Viceregal Lodge (above), which was built by Lord Dufferin in 1888. By 1903, there were 1,400 European homes on the hill top. Indians were only allowed to live on the lower slopes, described by Rudyard Kipling as "that crowded rabbit warren catering to the native population."

THE LIFE OF A MEMSAHIB

The English wives of British officers were known as memsahibs. They had many Indian servants in the house—an *ayah* to look after the children, cooks, tailors, maids, and gardeners. They spent their time trying to recreate, in India's unsuitable climate, the genteel English lives they had left behind.

A durzee (tailor) takes the memsahib's order

Indian silks were a great favorite with English ladies

Old Delhi is relegated to the background

Richly decorated elephants carry the new rulers

THE DELHI DURBAR, 1903

When Edward VII was crowned king of England in 1903, the Indian viceroy, Lord Curzon, organized a ceremony with much pomp and splendor, including an elephant procession through the streets of Delhi. Events like this were an ideal way to display the political might and glory of the British Empire to its Indian subjects.

The struggle for freedom

SIMPLICITY
Gandhi led a simple life. These sandals and a watch were among his few possessions.

AFTER THE REVOLT OF 1857 (p. 22), there were no major attacks on the British for some time. By the end of the 19th century, however, people had begun to resent colonial rule. Many Indians had heard about the French Revolution and the American Revolutionery War , and they too wanted their country to be free. At first, most people only wanted more rights within the colonial system, and the Indian National Congress was formed in 1885 to further this cause. Others wanted to violently overthrow the British, but their efforts met with little success. The real struggle for freedom began in 1915 when Mahatma Gandhi became the leader of the national movement. He believed in nonviolent resistance, or *satyagraha*. Inspired by him, millions of people took part in peaceful campaigns against foreign rule. This shook the Raj to its foundations. Weakened by World War II, Britain was forced to grant India independence in 1947.

Mahatma Gandhi

THE CHARKHA
The *charkha* (spinning wheel) became a symbol of national pride and self-reliance. Taxes imposed by the British government meant that imported cloth was cheaper than domestic, and the Indian textile workers suffered as a result.

THE SALT MARCH
Mohandas Karamchand Gandhi became known as The Mahatma (great soul) because of his enlightened, peaceful methods of resisting colonial rule. In 1930, Gandhi led a 200 mile (320 km)-long march to protest that salt, a basic human necessity, was being heavily taxed by the British. Thousands of supporters joined him on this Salt March, which became an important turning point in the freedom struggle. Although many were jailed for such "civil disobedience," they paved the way to freedom for India.

The dhoti *(a long, unstitched loincloth) always worn by Gandhi*

Indian women played an active role in the fight for India's freedom

INDIAN NATIONAL ARMY
Not everyone favored nonviolence. When World War II broke out in 1939, many Indians wanted to join forces with Britain's enemies to help throw the British out of the country. The Bengali leader, Subhash Chandra Bose, formed the Indian National Army with 20,000 men, who fought alongside invading Japanese forces. They were defeated, but in the process, further weakened Britain's power.

The jail is now a national monument

CELLULAR JAIL ANDAMAN ISLANDS
Hundreds of Indian freedom fighters were imprisoned by the British, and many died in terrible conditions in this jail, on a remote island in the Bay of Bengal.

"My religion is based on truth and nonviolence. Truth is my God. Nonviolence is the means of realizing Him."

MAHATMA GANDHI

Rich and poor people of all religions joined the Salt March

Gandhi was shot dead while on his way to a prayer meeting in Delhi

DEATH OF A STATESMAN
Gandhi opposed the division of India. Ironically, he was assassinated by a Hindu fanatic, Nathuram Godse, who resented Gandhi's concern for Muslims, whose leaders wanted a country of their own.

Free India

At the stroke of midnight, August 15 1947, British rule ended, and India became a free country. But along with the celebrations came great upheaval as the country itself was divided into two. The Muslim majority areas to the east and west became the new nation of Pakistan. This division, known as Partition, led to massive upheaval as Muslims moved to Pakistan, and Hindus and Sikhs fled to India. Millions were uprooted amidst violence and bloodshed. The interreligious hatred this caused was a source of great unhappiness to Jawaharlal Nehru, India's first prime minister, who supported Mahatma Gandhi's belief that all religious groups should be welcomed in India. The Constitution of India came into effect in 1950, and declared that all Indians, regardless of religion, caste, or creed, were equal citizens of the new republic. In 1952, India held the first of many general elections, and became the world's largest democracy, a title that it holds to this day.

RAISING THE FLAG
The Indian tricolor national flag was adopted in 1931 by the Indian National Congress party. The saffron denotes courage and sacrifice; the green, faith and charity. The wheel in the center represents the Hindu and Buddhist idea of *karma* – meaning that good deeds will be rewarded and bad ones punished.

LEADING THE WAY
Jawaharlal Nehru was leader of the Indian National Congress Party. He held the post of prime minister from 1947 until his death in 1964. When independence was finally declared, he made a brilliant speech, announcing that, "At the stroke of the midnight hour, when the world sleeps, India will awake to life and freedom."

TRANSFER OF POWER
Lord Mountbatten, Britain's viceroy, swears in Jawaharlal Nehru as India's first prime minister in a dramatic ceremony marking the end of British rule.

Thousands of refugees flee from their homes by crowding onto the tops of trains

MASS MIGRATION

Over 13 million people migrated across the newly created borders – Muslims to the new Islamic state of Pakistan, and Hindus to India. "A madness has seized the people," said Nehru as riots spread across the country. Angry at losing their homes and land, and fearful of the future, both sides attacked trains full of refugees and massacred their passengers.

Looking forward

United by a single constitution, which gave equal rights to all Indian citizens, the government of the newly independent nation set about trying to build a strong social and economic base. Education, social equality, agricultural reforms, and women's rights were all high on the agenda.

Regal elephants lead the parade

FRESHLY MINTED

The first coins and bills to be minted for the newly independent country came out exactly three years after independence was declared, on August 15, 1950. To this day, paper money still depicts Mahatma Gandhi, known to all as the "father of the nation."

The three-headed Ashokan lion is present on all coins and bills

SHOW OF STRENGTH

India declared itself a sovereign democratic republic on January 26, 1948. Every year on this day, a magnificent parade is held in New Delhi attended by the president, the prime minister, and other VIPs. Enthusiastic crowds watch as beautifully decorated elephants lead the parade of army, navy, and air force regiments as they march past to the rousing beat of military bands. Schoolchildren also dance and sing in the parade, and there's a procession of floats from each state. The grand finale is a dramatic flyby by air force fighter planes.

VOTING POWER

Every five years a general election is held to decide which of India's many political parties will come to power. Noisy, colorful election campaigns take place all over the country. Every Indian over the age of 18 is entitled to vote.

Heavy iron ballot box

ADULT LITERACY

One of Nehru's goals was to have 100 percent literacy in the country. Educational reforms and literacy programs have resulted in major improvements in literacy rates, but there is still some way to go before Nehru's dream can come true.

Life in the village

WATER FOR THE DAY
Water is scarce in remote villages, particularly those in arid areas where pipelines have not yet been laid. Women often have to walk for miles to collect water from the nearest well, which they carry home in brass pots on their heads.

THE VAST MAJORITY OF INDIANS still live in villages scattered throughout the country. Villagers depend on farming and on selling handmade goods, and life is largely determined by the changing of seasons, and the rhythm of sowing and harvesting. Village homes and crafts change from region to region, but there are certain sounds and sights typical of rural India— the smell of cow-dung smoke from cooking fires, children chasing cattle on dusty streets, women gathered around the village well, elders gossiping while resting on *charpais* (string cots) in the square. A village is usually a sprawling cluster of houses, crisscrossed by unpaved lanes, and surrounded by

fields. Life has an unhurried pace, with families carrying on traditions handed down over centuries, even though many of the younger generation have left for the cities in search of employment.

A mud-and-thatch hut is decorated with a simple design

A head at the end of the rod churns as it turns

THE BUTTER CHURN
This simple, homemade mechanism is a wooden rod turned using rope. Creamy milk from cows or buffaloes is collected in an earthenware pot and churned to make pure, white butter.

HEARTH AND HOME
Most village women cook outside, since their home is usually just one room. Food for the family is cooked using simple metal or clay pots on a *chulha* (stove) made of mud. Women frequently add fresh layers of mud in order to stop the stove from cracking.

Semiripened bananas are taken to market to be sold when ripe

Sheaves of wheat are carried on the head

The wind separates out the chaff from the grain

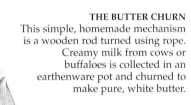

FRESH FROM THE FARM
Small farmers carry their own produce to a cooperative or joint outlet to be sold by wholesalers. They might also supply goods direct to their local market for sale.

BLOWING IN THE WIND
Farmers usually harvest two major crops a year–the *kharif* (winter) and the *rabi* (summer) crop. In north India, the winter crop is usually mustard and wheat, while in summer lentils are grown.

Slapping dung cakes on the wall

COW-DUNG CAKES
The cheapest and most easily made fuel for cooking in the village is the cow-dung cake. Villagers who own cattle collect cow-dung into heaps, bind it with straw, knead it into flat cakes, and slap them onto a plain surface to dry, before burning them along with wood.

LIVELY ENTERTAINMENT
These traveling musicians from Rajasthan wander from village to village with their instruments, performing on street corners or in courtyards. Their full-throated songs and tuneful folk music soon draw an enthusiastic crowd of listeners who give them money or food.

Beads and braids for adorning cattle, camels, and horses

Canvas sheets for makeshift stalls that can be quickly put up and taken down

MARKET DAY
Noisy and colorful markets (*haats*) are set up overnight in the village square. Normally these are weekly events, but they also spring up on festivals or religious holidays. Selling everything from livestock and farming equipment to kitchen utensils, clothes, and jewelry, the market is an ideal place to exchange news and gossip, to arrange marriages, or to discuss plans for the future. Bargaining to get the best price is a ritual that everyone enjoys.

Big cities

SOME OF THE WORLD'S LARGEST CITIES are in India. The most important of them correspond to the four points of the compass. In the north is Delhi; in the south is Chennai (Madras); to the west is Mumbai (Bombay), and to the east is Kolkata (Calcutta). The fast-growing cities of Bangalore and Hyderabad in the middle of the country form the heart of what is known as India's "silicon valley." Although over 70 percent of Indians still live in rural areas, urban centers are crowded, noisy, and colorful. Indian cities are full of contrasts. Here, past, present, and, future constantly collide. Bullock carts and elephants trundle past sleek, modern cars; skyscrapers soar above ramshackle slums; and old traditions rub shoulders with new technologies.

AT YOUR SERVICE
The first sight to greet a traveler at any big city railroad station is the uniformed *coolie*, or porter, who helps to carry luggage.

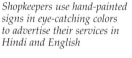

Shopkeepers use hand-painted signs in eye-catching colors to advertise their services in Hindi and English

LUMBERING ON
Alongside fast-moving traffic an elephant plods home after a full day at a city tourist sight.

JUICY PHONE CALL
Doubling up as a "public call office" (PCO), the fruit juice stall welcomes weary walkers in the city. Individual blends of fresh juice are made to order.

HIGH-TECH CITY, BANGALORE
Bangalore and Hyderabad are two of the fastest growing modern cities in India. They contain most of the country's computer industries and technology parks. Software programmers and developers from Bangalore often take up jobs in the US and Europe.

HIGH-RISE CITY, MUMBAI
Cities in India are growing at an alarming rate in terms of population, buildings, and traffic. Old buildings are being torn down to give way to high-rises as more and more people migrate to cities in search of work. Buildings and prices soar along the coastline of Mumbai, seen here. This is the home of the Hindi film industry, and many of the movie stars live in luxury high-rise apartments overlooking the sea.

CAPITAL CITY, DELHI
New Delhi, the capital of India, was designed by the British architect Edwin Lutyens in 1911 and took 20 years to complete. In contrast to New Delhi's wide, tree-lined avenues, the old part of the city is a maze of winding lanes and bustling bazaars.

A special spoon-like instrument is used to gently clean ears

Rashtrapati Bhawan, home of the president of India

ZIP CODES
Big cities are divided into zones, each with its own post code, or zip code. Red mailboxes are used for regular mail, whereas green ones are only for local mail within the city boundaries.

110092

LETTERS

PERSONAL ATTENTION
All sorts of services can be found on Indian city streets. People can get their shoes shined, their hair cut, or even have their ears cleaned – all on the way to work!

BARGAIN HUNTING
Away from stylish shopping centers are pavement stalls that sell all kinds of goods, from fish and vegetables to clothing, pots, and pans, all at bargain prices. Haggling for the best price is part of daily life for city shoppers.

STREET LIFE, KOLKATA
Buses, cars, trailers, trucks, scooters, three-wheelers, cycle-rickshaws, and bicycles make up the chaotic melée of traffic in the older parts of big cities. Auto rickshaw drivers honk their horns, cyclists clang their bells, the occasional bullock cart trundles by, and pedestrians somehow manage to zigzag their way across. In Kolkata, hand-pulled rickshaws are also used. To add to the chaos, cows are often found ambling through the traffic.

Hand-pulled rickshaw

SHARIFF'S GUEST HOUSE

Art and sculpture

Ceremonial fly whisk to cleanse the air

THERE IS A HUGE VARIETY of styles to be found in Indian art through the ages. Some artists, like the stone sculptors who carve divine figures on Hindu temples, continue a tradition unchanged for thousands of years. Other artists' styles changed with outside influences—from Persia and China, or later with the arrival of the Europeans. Gods and goddesses are the most common subjects, especially in the Hindu tradition. Although orthodox Islamic texts forbade the depiction of living creatures, the Mughal emperor Akbar argued that such paintings would deepen religious feeling. Under his patronage, the art of miniature painting flourished in the 17th century.

GLITTER FROM THE SOUTH
This art form, known as the Tanjore school of painting, uses a painted image as the base. Details are raised with plaster relief and decorated with brightly colored glass, semiprecious stones, and gold or silver leaf. The Raja of Thanjavur (Tanjore) in south India was its chief patron in the 18th century.

BIRD BY MANSUR
The Mughal emperor Shah Jahan's favorite painter was Mansur. His paintings of flowers, animals, birds like this goldfinch, were extremely detailed and lifelike.

PILLARS OF ART
The sensual curves of these divine figures are typical of many ancient Hindu temples. The female form of these *apsaras* (heavenly maidens) was thought to lift the human spirit toward a spiritual realization of god.

Gold leaf ornaments

Nandi, the holy bull, carries Shiva and Parvati on his back

TEMPLE EMBELLISHMENTS

The sponsors or patrons of temple art and sculpture were either royalty or the rich upper classes. This frieze decorates an 11th-century Jain temple near Jaipur. The Jains formed a wealthy merchant class who made generous donations to temples dedicated to their faith.

Jain saint attended by female celestial figures

Green parrots perch on the tree

Daubs of paint make up stylized flowers

FOLK PAINTING FROM BIHAR

Madhubani painting is a folk style from northern Bihar. Simple, colorful designs are created using vegetable dyes and black soot from cooking vessels. Instead of paintbrushes, the women artists use bamboo sticks.

Indian soldiers of the British Army

THE EUROPEANS ARRIVE

The British East India Company introduced the Company school of painting. This was a fusion between typical Indian styles, such as the flat, stylized patterns made by these marching soldiers, and Western subjects and characters.

WINGED HORSE

This beautiful flying horse is an example of *patachitra* (cloth painting) from the eastern state of Orissa. Images—usually of gods and goddesses, or mythical creatures—are painted on a particular kind of silk. They are made for pilgrims to take home from sacred sites.

The face is depicted with a gentle upward tilt

The left leg is always raised

Shiva is shown crushing evil

Delicately detailed trees and plants

PAINTING IN MINIATURE

Courtly life, wildlife, and natural scenes were captured in stylized detail in the miniature style of painting under the Mughals. Stories of the blue-skinned god Krishna were a favorite theme. Here he is playing his magic flute to enchant a group of village maidens. These tiny, intricate paintings are made using natural pigments made from minerals or plants. The brushes were so fine that sometimes one was made with just a single hair from a baby squirrel!

DANCING SHIVA

Shiva, the Destroyer, is shown in his well-known *tandava* (dance) pose. Religious texts prescribe the exact proportions, materials, and techniques for making these sacred south Indian metal images. If these rules are not observed, it is thought to bring bad luck to the artist or to the king.

Traditional craftwork

In India, many everyday objects are still made by hand, rather than by machines. Bags and baskets, pots and pans, shoes and toys are handcrafted by millions of artisans around the country. Most of them work in their village homes, or in tiny workshops in the cities. Traditional crafts vary from region to region, and use skills that have been handed down from one generation to the next. Wood, leather, terra-cotta, metal, and cloth are the most commonly used materials. From simple items such as water pots, to more decorative or ornamental pieces, Indian crafts are full of color and rich in detail.

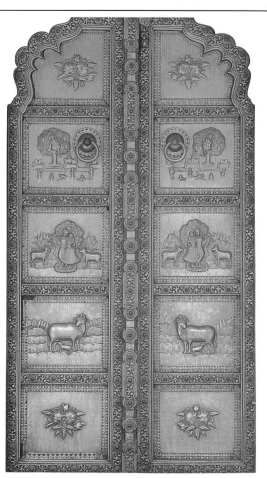

PUPPET HERO
Puppeteers usually make their own puppets out of wood and cloth. Familiar tales of folk heroes and their adventures are enacted by traveling puppeteers on makeshift stages. Puppet shows draw large audiences of adults as well as children.

Silk frill for added decoration

FANCY FAN
The fine gold thread work on this antique fan shows that embroidery was not used for just decorating clothes. Chair covers, table linen, and fans like this one were richly embroidered in silver and gold thread. The owner of this fan was probably a member of the royalty. The fan is twirled around its wooden handle to create a cool breeze.

Gold embroidery over cotton padding creates a 3D effect

EMBOSSED BRASS
Old windows and doors in metal or wood display the tremendous versatility of the Indian craftsman. He works as skillfully on large objects as on smaller decorative pieces. A huge, ornate door in the Jaipur City Palace is made of two large sheets of brass embossed wih symbols of Lord Krishna.

Wood is carved, brightly painted, and lacquered

WORKING WITH LEATHER
Almost every Indian village has a local cobbler, who makes sturdy leather sandals (*chappals*) for everyday wear. For special occasions, more elaborate decorations are stitched on to pointed slip-on shoes called *jootis*. Horse and camel saddles are also richly decorated by leather workers.

Jootis are made of locally cured leather

A SAFE SWING
Seated on a toy *jhoola* (swing), this little doll is dressed in a traditional sari and blouse. The woodcarvers who make these toys also make full-size swings that can sometimes be found hanging from the roof beams in old houses.

Perforated lid allows rosewater to come through

Fine details are painted on with a Pashmina goat's hair

PAPIER MACHÉ
Kashmir, in the north of India, is famous for intricately painted papier maché. Plates, vases, boxes, Christmas decorations, and numerous other objects are made from paper mulch and glue. The entire surface is then covered with painted designs of birds, animals, flowers, and plants.

HAIRPIN
This antique brass hairpin can also be used as a comb. Hair dressing was given great importance in ancient times, and Indian women still wear all kinds of decorative clips, slides, and even flowers in their hair.

BASKETRY
All over India, baskets are woven from bamboo, which is both flexible and resilient. This conical basket is used by tea pickers for collecting leaves.

Smooth lip so that the water could be poured without spilling

TEA CONTAINER
Locally called a *dongmo*, this bamboo and brass container is used by north Indian hill folk to brew tea.

COLORFUL METAL
This long-stemmed rosewater sprinkler is a 19th century example of the art of enameling (*meenakari*), particularly popular in the western province of Rajasthan. Grooves are cut into the metal and filled with enamel to create colorful patterns. *Meenakari* is often used to make earrings and necklaces. It was introduced in the 16th century by the royal family of Jaipur who brought the first five Sikh enamel workers to India from Lahore.

Blue and green enamel on brass

SILVER GIANT
Silver was used to create a variety of vessels. This is one of a pair of gigantic urns made by the Maharaja of Jaipur, Madho Singh II, so that he could carry a six-month supply of sacred Ganges water with him when he visited London in 1901. These are the largest silver objects in the world, 5.24 ft (1.6 m) tall. Each of the urns could hold 2,160 gallons of water.

Jewelry

Gems inlaid into the metal band

IN INDIA, JEWELRY IS NOT ONLY decorative, it also has symbolic value. The nine major gemstones, for example, each signify a particular planet: rubies for the sun, pearls for the moon, emeralds for mercury, coral for mars, topaz for jupiter, diamonds for venus, and sapphires for saturn. Tiger's eye and zircon represent the ascending and descending positions of the planets. These nine stones are known collectively as *navaratna* and are worn to promote good health or avert bad luck. During the Mughal period, the arts of *kundan* (setting gems in narrow, layered strips of pure gold) and *meenakari* (enameling) were perfected. The most lavish example is Shah Jahan's fabled Peacock Throne which was set with 108 rubies and 1.13 tons (1,150 kgs) of gold! Gold is regarded as a symbol of life and of purity, and is always worn by Indian brides.

Droplet made of glass

ALL THAT GLITTERS
For those who can't afford gold and precious gems, these silver earrings are just as eye-catching. Instead of jewels they are set with pieces of blue glass.

Silver stud worn in the nose

Ivory, from elephants' tusks, is no longer used

CASKET OF JEWELS
Jewelry boxes are often as intricate and beautiful as the jewels they store. This 19th-century casket from south India is made of sandalwood and decorated tortoiseshell inlay. The ivory panels are etched with images of two Hindu goddesses.

Beaded headdress

Hollow silver neck band

TRIBAL JEWELRY
This young tribal girl from Kutchch in western India is wearing traditional Rajasthani jewelry. In this part of India, any spare money is often invested in jewelry, so women literally wear their wealth.

Sequins are used instead of jewels

Elephant with short, upturned trunk

COLORFUL BANGLES
Bangles come in many different styles. Brightly colored, inexpensive bangles made from glass or papier maché and paste are worn particularly during the festival season; enameled ones are for other special occasions. Gold bangles symbolize a woman's married status. These could be plain circlets or elaborate filigree bands with animal-head decorations.

Gold bangles with elephant head terminals

Peacocks are a symbol of royalty

PEACOCKS AND PEARLS
This pendant from south India is called a *padakkam*. It is studded with emeralds, rubies, and diamonds and set in gold.

Pearls hang like water droplets from a flower

A COLLAR FOR A QUEEN
This uniquely Indian form of rigid necklace is known as a *hasli* because it rests on the collarbone (*hansuli*). The basic shape is cast in gold, and then etched with patterned grooves. The enamel colors are ground, mixed to a paste, painted in the grooves, and heated so that they fuse before the stones are finally set.

Goldsmith blows down tube to stoke the fire

SMELTING GOLD
Traditional goldsmiths use a primitive iron tube and mud oven to melt metal ore and remove all its impurities. They use hammers and chisels to work the pure gold that is left into all manner of intricate ornaments.

Chain hooks behind ear

Chain with a pendant worn along the hair parting is called a mang tika *or* tikli

Sapphire, cut so that it sparkles

Heavy, gold pendant

GEMSTONES
In India, gemstones are thought to have certain healing properties. Sapphires are believed to be the most powerful.

Nine auspicious planetary stones

Meenakari *peacock dancing*

FLIP FLOP
Kundan and *meenakari* feature on each side of the same pendant. The front is studded with jewels while the back is beautifully enameled.

Glass bangles interspersed with gold ones

The hathphool *("hand flower") is a bracelet linked by gold chains to rings on her fingers*

BEJEWELED BRIDE
An Indian woman usually wears more jewelry than a Western woman, but on her wedding day she is covered in beautiful gold and jewels. Each ornament worn by a bride underlines her new status as a married woman and signifies her faithfulness to her husband. Traditionally, the only wealth a woman has of her own is the jewelry she receives when she gets married.

Anklet with silver bells

Toe ring

41

The literary tradition

STORYTELLING IN INDIA is an art. For centuries, tales of folklore and religion were passed down by word of mouth. That is why every Indian knows the two great epics—the *Mahabharata* and *Ramayana*—though few have read them in full. When they were written down in manuscript form, artists illustrated each page so that it looked like a painting. Traditional plays, such as those written in Sanskrit by Kalidas in the 4th century AD, continue to be read and performed. The Mughals introduced Persian calligraphy (beautiful writing) to record the lives of their monarchs. Under the British Raj, the novel and short story became popular. India's most famous writer, Rabindranath Tagore, wrote prose and poetry, and was awarded the Nobel Prize for Literature in 1913. Each regional language has its own literary tradition. English, too, has become an official Indian language, and is used by many writers today.

STORY BOX
The *kavad* is a storehouse of tales. It represents the ancient tradition of telling stories through pictures. Unlatch the storyteller's stomach and its hinged doors unfold to depict scenes from popular folklore. Hindus believe that the god Vishnu is reborn 10 times—the seventh time as Krishna (on the left panel), and the eighth as Ram (on the right), hero of the epic *Ramayana*.

BARK SCROLL
Before the 16th century, scribes wrote on strips of bark, or on palm leaves, instead of paper.

CHRONICLES AND CALLIGRAPHY
The art of calligraphy flourished under the Mughals. Apart from writing out the Koran in Arabic or Persian, the Mughals also chronicled the lives of their royalty, and even wrote recipe books. In the 17th century, birds and animals, like this rhino, were "drawn" by using letters, words, or phrases from poems or religious texts. The loops, squiggles, and dots of the Naksh script, seen here, are used to suggest the animal's shape and features.

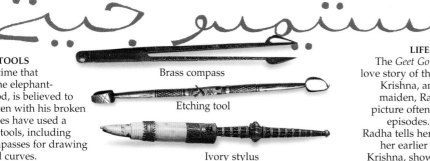

SCRIBE'S TOOLS
Since the time that Ganesh, the elephant-headed god, is believed to have written with his broken tusk, scribes have used a variety of tools, including metal compasses for drawing circles and curves.

Brass compass

Etching tool

Ivory stylus

LIFE OF KRISHNA
The *Geet Govinda* tells the love story of the Hindu god, Krishna, and a beautiful maiden, Radha. A single picture often contains two episodes. On the right, Radha tells her friend about her earlier meeting with Krishna, shown on the left.

The marriage of Ram and Sita

Ram and his brother meet the bird who saw Sita being kidnapped by the demon king

PICTORIAL GUIDE
The teachings of the 10 Sikh gurus are written in Gurmukhi in this beautifully illustrated book, the *Dasam Granth*. The Gurmukhi script is used for Punjabi, a north Indian language.

NOBEL LAUREATE
Rabindranath Tagore wrote in Bengali, one of India's 18 regional languages. The collection of poems, *Gitanjali*, is his most famous work. He was also an artist, musician, and educator.

Woman holding up her long hair

RECORD OF DAILY LIFE
Some people had a flair for recording even common everyday activities that took place in the village. Basic text accompanied the drawings. The picture on the left of this book, made from handmade paper, shows a man having an oil massage, and on the right shows a woman bathing, while her friend hides her with a veil.

Most major religious texts were written in Sanskrit

The lovers meet in an enchanted garden

Radha tells a friend about her earlier meeting with Krishna

Music

MUSIC IS AN INTEGRAL PART of all worship and celebration in India. Ancient hymns are chanted at ceremonies. Roadside stalls blare out film songs. Music concerts—both classical and pop—attract huge crowds. India's classical music tradition goes back thousands of years. It is divided into two branches: Hindustani classical music in the north, and Karnataka music in the south. Both are based on *raga* (melody) and *taal* (rhythm). There are hundreds of *ragas* that evoke different moods, seasons, and times of day. They can be sung as well as played on instruments such as the sitar. Each region also has its own treasury of folk songs. But the most popular songs throughout the country are from Hindi films, and these are hummed and sung by almost everyone.

KRISHNA AND HIS FLUTE
Lord Krishna is said to have been brought up as a cowherd who played his magic flute in the meadows of Vrindavan, a little town in north India.

THE MAESTRO
Ravi Shankar popularized the sound of the sitar in the West. He composed and played *ragas* with famous musicians, such as the violinist, Yehudi Menuhin.

Black tuning disk to give harmonic overtones

DRUMMING SUPPORT
The *tabla* is one of a pair of drums that provides the rhythm in Hindustani classical music. The *tabla* (right) is tuned to the upper tonic note of the *raga*, while the *bayan* (left) sounds the lower note. Both together maintain the beat. The *tabla* player hits the center of the drum skin with his fingers and presses down with the heel of his palm to vary the pitch.

Drum carved out of solid hard wood

Hollow drum made of copper, brass, bronze, or clay

Arched metal frets

Soundbox made from a hollow gourd

Ivory bridge

SITAR STRINGS
The *sitar* is the most important instrument in north Indian classical music, and is one of several such stringed instruments. The *sitar* usually has seven main strings and about a dozen "sympathetic strings" beneath the convex metal frets along the hollow neck. These vibrate spontaneously when the main strings are played, adding a layer of shimmering sound.

Sitar players' fingertips are tough and calloused from pressing down on the metal strings

Decorated hollow gourd resonates with sound

Painted bamboo tube

Wooden tuning peg

DIVINE VEENA
Stringed instruments give the rippling, droning sound characteristic of Indian classical music. The most ancient of these is the *veena*. It has seven strings, a large resonating bowl made from a hollow gourd under each end of the body, and movable metal frets on a bamboo tube. Four of the seven strings are fingered to create the melody, which is varied by plucking the other three strings. The *veena* is mainly used in south Indian classical music.

Drone string is one of seven strings

Metal frets determine the notes

The been is a reed instrument played by snake charmers

Singer clasps her hand to her ear

WOMEN MUSICIANS
These 19th-century ivory figurines show women musicians from Maharashtra in western India, a region renowned for its classical music tradition. Women have been at the forefront of both north and south Indian music. While women do play instruments, the majority are singers. In classical Indian music, the human voice is superior to instruments.

Tambourine

Emperor Akbar

Tansen

Guru Haridas

GODDESS OF MUSIC
Saraswati, the Hindu goddess of music and learning, is often shown playing the *veena*.

TANSEN, THE LEGEND
Tansen was the most famous musician of the Mughal period. He was court musician to Emperor Akbar and was trained by the legendary music teacher, Guru Haridas. Tansen's singing was so powerful it was said that he could make the sun come out, bring on the rain, or even light a lamp with his beautiful voice.

Classical dance

THERE ARE FIVE MAJOR SCHOOLS of Indian classical dance. Each form has a distinct style, expression, and costume, and they all depict stories from the ancient myths and epics. Bharata Natyam is the oldest classical form, and is based on a dance manual called *Natya Shastra* written in AD 200. The dancer aims to combine symmetry and sharp angles with softness and grace. This dance form originated in Tamil Nadu. The neighboring state of Kerala gave rise to Kathakali—a spectacular dance-drama, for which the dancers wear elaborate costumes and facepaint. The color of the dancer's face depends on whether he is playing an evil or heroic character: green faces for heroes and jet black for villains. The gentler, lyrical style of Odissi dance originated in the temples of Orissa in eastern India. Manipuri is the equally graceful dance form of India's northeastern states. Kathak, on the other hand, has rapid, rhythmic footwork and spins. It is a north Indian dance form that was very popular in the royal courts of the Mughals.

DANCING SHIVA
In Hindu legend, dance originated with Lord Shiva, in the form of Nataraja, the "Lord of Dance." His *tandava* dance represents the destruction and recreation of the universe. Dancing in a ring of flames, he crushes forces of evil under his feet.

Left hand depicts the Ganges River flowing from Shiva's hair

Right hand depicts the matted locks of Lord Shiva

Cymbals are made of brass and lightly engraved

The skirt is made up of many layers of white cotton

KEEPING THE RHYTHM
A small group of musicians on the dancer's stage often includes a player, who claps the cymbals to provide emphasis to the narration which is sung.

STRENGTH AND GRACE
The word "bharata" is made up of *bhava* (expression), *raga* (melody), and *taal* (rhythm), the three key components of Bharata Natyam. The dancer's hand gestures convey specific meanings. She shows how the sacred Ganges River was born from the matted hair of the Hindu god, Lord Shiva.

Silk sari

Gold pendant, studded with semiprecious stones

Belt holds the sari firmly in place

Pleats fan out for ease of movement

JINGLE BELLS
Ghungroos are brass bells worn around the ankles. They jingle in time with the dancer's steps, and help keep the beat.

Ghungroos

DANCE, DRAMA, AND STAMINA

Kathakali dance is almost like a martial art. Dancers have to undergo years of rigorous training to build up their stamina and flexibility. Every part of the body and face (even the eyes) are exercised, and every nerve, joint, and muscle toned to perfection. Only men become Kathakali dancers, so female roles are also played by them. The dramatic face makeup takes several hours to complete, ending with a small seed placed in the eye that turns the whites to red. Performances often continue throughout the night.

Intricate eye movements are essential to Kathakali

The faces of royal, divine, or heroic characters are painted green

Red clothes are worn by noble characters

The dancer's feet are stained bright red

LIVING SCULPTURE

The classical dance of Orissa, known as Odissi, dates back to the 2nd century AD. With her weight on one leg accentuating the curve of her waist, this dancer looks like a beautiful temple sculpture brought to life.

A lehenga (skirt) swirls around with the dancer's movements

Churidar (tight leggings)

SWIRLS AND SPINS

Kathak is the only classical dance form of north India. Under the patronage of the Mughals, Kathak moved from the temple courtyard to the royal court. Apart from royalty, the nobility and upper classes would regularly hold Kathak performances at home for their personal entertainment, showering favorite dancers with expensive gifts and jewels.

Mouthwatering cuisine

MOST WESTERNERS USED TO THINK that Indian food could be summed up in one word: curry. The word "curry" is thought to have come from the Tamil "*kari*" meaning sauce. In fact, there's such a huge variety of different types of Indian cooking, it would be difficult to taste them all in a single lifetime. Each region has its own style of cooking. When the Mughals came to India from Afghanistan and the Middle East, they brought with them exotic spices, dried fruits, and nuts, which flavor the rich, creamy sauce of "Mughlai" dishes. Kashmir is famous for its subtle *kormas*, and fragrant rice *pulaos*. In the south, the dominant flavors are coconut and curry leaves. Hindus rarely eat beef, since they consider the cow to be sacred. In fact, many are pure vegetarians. Muslims, on the other hand, do not eat pork.

Dal, a kind of lentil soup

TINGLING TASTEBUDS
Roadside stalls sell a mouth-watering array of tangy snacks. *Chaat* is a catch-all term for a variety of snacks made from potato, chick peas, crisp fried shells called *papdis,* topped with sweet and sour chutneys. *Gol gappas* (potato-stuffed *puris* dipped in tamarind water) are a real mouthful!

Panch phoron is a blend of five different seeds and spices

Etchings of Persian calligraphy

Tandoori roti (unleavened bread)

MASALA MIX
The magic of Indian cooking lies in the combinations of spices (*masalas*) used. These can be used whole or ground into powder.

COOKING UP A FEAST
Large vessels, such as this Mughal-era copper pot, are used both for cooking and for serving. The lid would be sealed using bread dough, and the rice, meat and spices inside would be steamed. This kind of cooking is called *dum pukht* and was invented by the Muslim rulers of Lucknow in the 19th century.

Tomato chutney

Coconut chutney

Coriander sauce

Heavy brass rolling pin

Sambhar, a spicy lentil and tomato soup

Dosa, a thin, folded pancake

Idlis (steamed rice cakes)

ROLLING A ROTI
Every Indian kitchen has a *chakla-belan* (rolling pin and base) on which balls of dough are rolled out to make flat, round *rotis,* which are then cooked on a flat *tawa* (griddle) on a hot fire.

MEAL ON A LEAF
Dosas are a staple food for south Indians. Made with ground rice flour, these thin crispy pancakes come with little side dishes of chutney, and are often stuffed with mashed vegetables and onions. *Dosas* are fried on a large, flat iron skillet, and are best eaten piping hot. Instead of a plate, they are served on a single large banana leaf.

Spicy chicken cooked in a kadhai (wok)

Malai kofta, vegetable dumplings in a creamy gravy

TANDOOR
A *tandoor* is a kind of clay oven, filled with burning embers. Tandoori cooking is very popular in north India. Chunks of meat are skewered and grilled in the fire, while flat bread bakes on the inside of the *tandoor*.

Chicken chunks marinated and flame-grilled

Mixed vegetables

ON A SILVER PLATTER
Traditional Indian meals are served on a *thali* (platter of silver or steel), with small bowls of vegetables, *dal* (lentils) and *curd* (yogurt). Rice, *rotis*, pickles, and *papads* are added to make it as complete a meal as possible, often rounded off with Indian confectioneries. The nice thing about a *thali* is that you can mix and match the different flavors, so that each mouthful is a different tasty experience.

Leaves are stuffed and rolled up ready to eat

Raita, a yogurt, cucumber, and tomato salad

Betel leaf

Papads, deep-fried chips

Saffron is used for yellow color

Plain, boiled rice offsets all the other rich flavors

Confectioneries are deep fried, then soaked in sugar syrup

FOR A SWEET TOOTH
Indian confectioneries are usually very sweet. Mostly made from milk products, some are served with generous helpings of sugary syrup.

Gulab Jamun

Kesar phirni

Milky pudding

...AND TO FINISH
Nothing rounds off a full Indian meal like a mouthful of paan. This after-dinner digestive is made from fine slivers of betel nut mixed with grated coconut, edible lime, aniseed, and sometimes sugar. The mixture is then folded inside a fresh betel leaf and popped into the mouth to cleanse the palate and freshen the breath.

Animal kingdom

ANIMALS THAT IN many countries are seen only in zoos still roam free in the jungles of India. Although huge tracts of forest have been cleared to provide land for farming, a great variety of wildlife still survives. To help preserve these species, national parks and sanctuaries have been established. The Gir National Park in western India is home to the rare Asiatic lion. Tigers, leopards, and vast numbers of deer, monkeys, reptiles, and exotic birds are found inside, and even occasionally outside, these protected areas. Some animals such as snakes, monkeys, elephants, cows, and even mice, are considered by Hindus to be sacred.

Bright green feathers of the Indian parakeet

PRETTY POLLY
Jewel-bright parakeets are a common sight in Indian cities, orchards, and woodlands. They eat fruit and nuts which they crack with their powerful beaks. This colorful bird is a plum-headed parakeet.

ON THE LOOKOUT
India is home to many species of deer. These elegant, shy chital (or axis deer) are very common, whereas the tiny mouse deer, which is only 1 ft (30 cms) high, is very difficult to spot.

THE LAST MAIL?
These postage stamps show two of India's endangered species: the blood pheasant on the right, and the markhor on the left. They are a reminder of how important it is to protect the natural environment so that such species do not become extinct.

LORD OF THE JUNGLE
At one time, India's forests were home to hundreds of thousands of tigers. Now, this magnificent animal can be found in just a few protected reserves in the country. The most feared of all jungle predators, the tiger has in turn been ruthlessly hunted by man. Trade in tiger skins is now banned worldwide, and poaching is strictly illegal. However, a greater threat now comes from pollution, and the destruction of the forests where these beautiful creatures live.

Peacock tail
feather

AN EVENING DRINK BY THE RIVER

Wild Indian elephants live in large herds, gathering by the water's edge each evening to drink and bathe. Each herd of females and young is led by one dominant female, while the males, or tuskers, are solitary. Elephants are generally peaceful creatures but, if threatened, can charge at tremendous speed.

PROUD AS A PEACOCK

India's national bird, the peacock, is best known for its gorgeous tail feathers, which are sometimes used (illegally) to make fans and ornaments. The colorful males and dusky brown females are very common in rural areas, and are even seen in cities throughout the country.

Elephants suck up water in their long trunks

Long, tufted tail

Cobras can grow to 16 ft (5 m) long

Hood is spread ready to strike

MONKEY GOD

Hindus consider monkeys sacred because of their association with Hanuman, the monkey god. He is renowned for being brave, agile, strong and, above all, extremely loyal. Rhesus monkeys make the most of this reputation, gathering near Hanuman temples to be fed by devotees.

DEADLY CHARMERS

One of India's deadliest snakes is the cobra. It prepares to strike by spreading out the ribs on either side of its head in a "hood." The cobra's natural enemy is the mongoose, which grabs the snake's head in its sharp teeth.

LOST RHINO

Kaziranga, in the eastern state of Assam, is the only place where the magnificent one-horned Indian rhino is still found in the wild. Its massive bulk and "armor-plated" skin make it look like a dinosaur. In fact, it has changed little in the last million years.

Science and technology

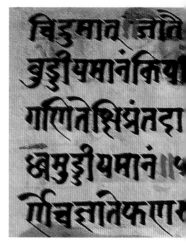

MANY PEOPLE THINK OF INDIA as a land of religion and superstition, but the country has also produced eminent scientists through the ages. Perhaps India's greatest contribution to mathematics is the invention of zero. Arab traders who introduced these numerals to Europe even referred to mathematics as "the Indian art." The most famous scientist of ancient India was Aryabhatta (AD 476–500), who correctly calculated the circumference of the earth, discovered the cause of solar and lunar eclipses, and stated that the earth rotates around the sun. In the 12th century, the mathematician Bhaskaracharya further developed the concepts of zero and infinity. Since the 1980s, India has led the field in the computing industry. Highly skilled engineers and programmers from India can now be found across the world, especially in the US.

Iron pillar in Delhi's Qutb Minar complex

RUSTLESS LUSTER
Metallurgy was an advanced science as early as the 4th century AD when this iron pillar was cast. Made as a flagstaff honoring the god Vishnu, it remains to this day unblemished by rust.

Needle points to the various stars and planets

MAP OF THE STARS
A brass globe from 1629 is engraved with the positions of the stars and planets. The writing is in Persian.

POCKET GUIDE
An astrolabe is a two-dimensional map of the sky. This brass one was brought to India in the 13th century by Arab astronomers.

OBSERVING THE SKIES
The Jantar Mantar observatory in Jaipur was built in 1734 and is the largest of the five observatories built by Jai Singh II during his reign. An avid astronomer, he built gigantic instruments as big as buildings by which he could calculate the exact position of planets, and forecast the timing of solar and lunar eclipses. Some instruments were also used to predict the arrival of the monsoon rains, or forecast how hot the coming summer months would be.

Stairway to the top of the sundial

Each of the 12 main pieces represents a sign of the zodiac

ADVANCED MATHEMATICS
Written in Sanskrit by the famous mathematician Bhaskaracharya (b. AD 1114), the *Lilawati* manuscript uses pictures of birds and animals to explain difficult concepts such as trigonometry. Here, two monkeys are shown walking toward an acute angle. Elsewhere, a peacock swoops down to catch a snake in its beak, at a perfect right angle!

The monkeys' pathways meet at a 45° angle

Lower monkey walks along the base of the triangle

India's first wholly-owned satellite launch vehicle blasted off in April 2001, sending a communications satellite into orbit

"We do not have the fantasy of competing with economically advanced nations in the exploration of the moon ... (But) we must be second to none in the application of advanced technologies to the real problems of man and society."

DR. VIKRAM SARABHAI

THE RAMAN EFFECT
Professor C.V. Raman (1888-1970) founded the Indian Academy of Sciences. He received the Nobel Prize for Physics in 1930 for discovering that light scatters when it passes through transparent material. This is called the Raman effect.

A sadhu (holy man) uses a laptop to compute horoscopes

ROCKETING FORWARD
In the 1960s, India's ambitious space program was launched by Dr. Vikram Sarabhai. The first of many satellites, Aryabhatta (named after ancient India's greatest scientist), was put into orbit in 1975. In 1992, the first of the new generation of INSAT satellites was launched. These are used to monitor changes in the climate, to survey for minerals and other natural resources, and for the latest telecommunications.

BYTES OF KNOWLEDGE
Since the late 1980s, India has invested heavily in computer education. IT and computer courses are offered in thousands of institutes across the country, and India's Institutes of Information Technology are among the world's finest. India now has among the largest number of software professionals in the world. Even in rural areas, laptops are used to find out crop prices and weather forecasts from the internet.

Religion and beliefs

FOLLOWERS OF ALMOST EVERY RELIGION can be found in India. Four major world religions—Hinduism, Buddhism, Jainism, and Sikhism—originated here. While over 80 percent of Indians practice some form of Hinduism, the country has one of the largest Muslim populations in the world. Sikhs make up about two percent of the population, and mainly come from the northern state of Punjab. There are almost as many Christians in India as there are Sikhs, and they have thrived in south India since Christ's apostle St. Thomas came to India in the 1st century AD. People who follow the Zoroastrian faith are known as Parsis. This small, but distinct, religious community lives in the western state of Maharashtra and in the city of Mumbai. Buddhism is largely confined to the mountainous regions of Ladakh and Sikkim, where the landscape is dotted with monasteries and prayer flags.

SOUND OF THE SHELL
The conch shell is blown to mark the start of most Hindu rituals.

ZOROASTER
Parsis are followers of the Persian prophet Zoroaster (1500–1000 BC), and they believe that fire is sacred. This image is of a *fravashi*, or guardian spirit, and represents the good in people.

THE SOUND OF THE INFINITE
The syllable OM or AUM signifies God, the everlasting. It is said or sung before and after all Hindu prayers. Repeated chanting of OM is said to bring about a feeling of serenity and peace.

Ganesh's half halo is a sign of his divine status

He holds a stylized conch shell in one of his four hands

An ornamental mace represents self-control

A sweet called a laddoo is Ganesh's favorite food

Piece of broken tusk which he used to write with instead of a pen

ELEPHANT GOD GANESH
One of the favorite Hindu gods is Ganesh, the firstborn son of Shiva and Parvati. According to Hindu mythology, Shiva cut off his son's head in a fit of anger but, seeing his wife's grief, brought him back to life by replacing the boy's head with that of an elephant. Ganesh is the god of wisdom; he also brings good luck and is known as "the remover of obstacles." He is especially honored in the western state of Maharashtra during an annual 10-day festival known as Ganesh Chaturthi.

HOLY BOOK OF THE SIKHS

The Guru Granth Sahib is the Sikh scripture, written in verse by Guru Nanak, founder of Sikhism, and nine other gurus (spiritual guides). The book occupies a central place in the *gurudwara* (temple). The priest fans it with a ceremonial whisk, as a mark of respect. Sikhism places great importance on the need for spiritual guides who help their followers along the spiritual path. The word "Sikh" actually means "disciple."

Ceremonial fly whisk

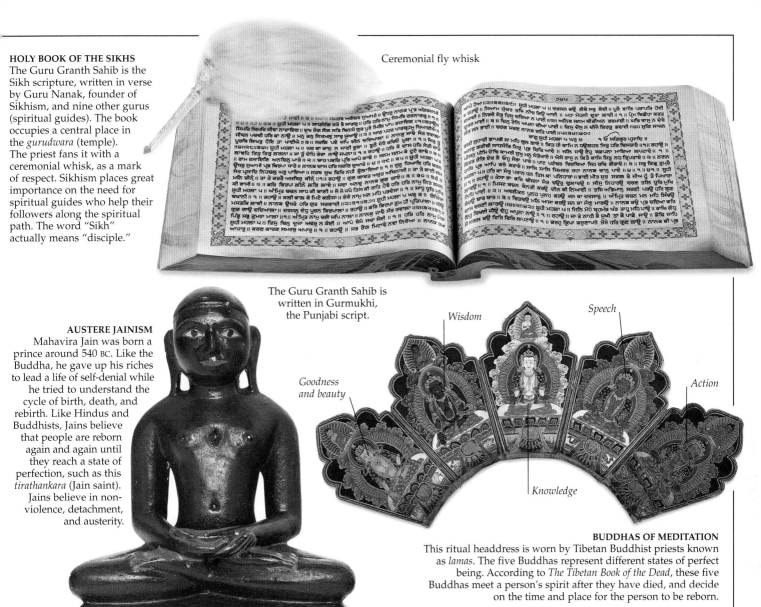

The Guru Granth Sahib is written in Gurmukhi, the Punjabi script.

AUSTERE JAINISM

Mahavira Jain was born a prince around 540 BC. Like the Buddha, he gave up his riches to lead a life of self-denial while he tried to understand the cycle of birth, death, and rebirth. Like Hindus and Buddhists, Jains believe that people are reborn again and again until they reach a state of perfection, such as this *tirathankara* (Jain saint). Jains believe in non-violence, detachment, and austerity.

Wisdom

Speech

Goodness and beauty

Action

Knowledge

BUDDHAS OF MEDITATION

This ritual headdress is worn by Tibetan Buddhist priests known as *lamas*. The five Buddhas represent different states of perfect being. According to *The Tibetan Book of the Dead*, these five Buddhas meet a person's spirit after they have died, and decide on the time and place for the person to be reborn.

MOTHER AND CHILD

Paintings and statues of the Virgin Mary, mother of Jesus Christ, are found in all churches in India. Indian Christians can be either Roman Catholic or Protestant. The largest Christian communities are found in the southwestern states of Kerala, where most people are Syrian Christians, and Goa, with its magnificent Portuguese cathedrals.

The infant Jesus in the arms of the Virgin Mary

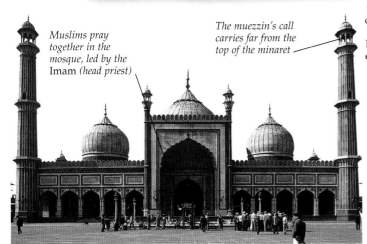

Muslims pray together in the mosque, led by the Imam (head priest)

The muezzin's call carries far from the top of the minaret

CALL OF THE MUEZZIN

In Islam, the call to prayer (*azan*) is made five times a day by a mosque official, called the *muezzin*, from one of the minarets in a mosque. prayers are offered facing Mecca, indicated by a niche in the wall which is called a *mihrab*. Followers of Islam are called Muslims, or "those who surrender to the will of God." Islam teaches that there is only one God, Allah, and that his prophet is Muhammad. The "five pillars" of Islam are: prayer, fasting, charity, confession of faith, and pilgrimage.

Rites and rituals

IN INDIA, RITES AND RITUALS mark every stage of an individual's life from birth to death. Each community and region has its own special variations. There are special ceremonies not only for the birth and naming of children, but even when they eat their first grain of rice (*annaprashan*), or when they write their first letter of the alphabet. The initiation of boys and girls into the faith of their community – Hindu, Muslim, Sikh, or Jain – is also a significant moment. Weddings are perhaps the most important and colorful event, when friends and family from far and wide come together for several days of feasting and celebration. When they die, Hindus are usually cremated and their ashes scattered in the sacred Ganges River.

Butter-filled cups waiting to be lit

Brass pot holds sacred water

FIRE AND WATER
To mark the start of a ritual, butter lamps are lit and the air is purified by sprinkling holy Ganges water.

PRAYING WITH FLOWERS
Almost all Hindu rituals use flowers. When someone dies, little boats made of dried leaves filled with marigolds and rose petals are set adrift on the Ganges River.

FIRST WORDS
For the Bengalis of east India, learning to write is an important moment in a child's life. The first letter of the alphabet is drawn in rice grains and Saraswati, the goddess of learning, is invoked.

A bridesmaid showers the happy couple with flower petals

MARRIAGE CEREMONY
This painting, in the traditional folk style called Madhubani, depicts a Hindu marriage ceremony. The bride is wearing lots of jewelry, including a heavy nose-ring, earrings, and bangles. Before the wedding, an Indian bride takes a ritual bath, and her feet and hands are painted with henna. Gifts are exchanged between the two families, and the celebrations continue for several days. The bride and groom garland each other with flowers. The high point of the ceremony comes when they walk together around a sacred fire seven times, while the priest chants sacred Sanskrit texts.

Pot of sacred Ganges water

The bride and groom exchange flower garlands

HONORING A SAINT

Coins collect in the center

This colorful cloth, known as a *chador*, is considered sacred, and is brought out for special Muslim festivals, such as the birthday of a saint. Volunteers parade the *chador* around the streets collecting offerings of money and flowers. For the rest of the year, it covers the shrine inside the grounds of the mosque. The *chador* itself is sometimes given as an offering, in thanks for a prayer which has been answered or as a mark of devotion.

Thread symbolizes universal fellowship

BROUGHT INTO THE FOLD

Parsi boys between the ages of seven and twelve are initiated into the Zoroastrian faith in a ceremony known as Navjote. They are dressed in white, to symbolize purity and renewal, and are given a sacred thread, or *kushti*, made of 72 strands twisted together. There is a similar ceremony for girls, where they are ritually dressed in saris.

BIRTH CERTIFICATE

Every newborn child has his or her horoscope cast. This decorative scroll is an astrological chart showing the position of the planets that will govern the child's life. It is unique to each person. Prospective brides and grooms will always check their partner's chart to make sure it is compatible with their own.

Symbols show the positions of the planets at the exact time of birth

Parchment scroll

Pilgrims face toward the sun to offer up their prayers

Sunlight passes through the water as it is offered back to the river

TAKING A HOLY DIP

Hindus believe that bathing in the Ganges River will wash away the sins not only of this lifetime, but of lifetimes to come. Along the banks of the river, ancient towns like Haridwar, Rishikesh, and Varanasi flourished as sacred centers for pilgrims wanting to cleanse themselves in the holy water. Sadhus (holy men) sit on the steps leading down to the river, and are paid to perform certain rituals on behalf of the pilgrims who come there. Many people fill brass pots with holy water to take back home with them.

Festivals

INDIA IS A LAND OF FESTIVALS. Hardly a month passes by without a festival being celebrated somewhere in the country. In the north, the high point of the year comes after the long, hot summer, with the festivals of Dusshera, Durga Puja, and Diwali. The other big festival, Holi, comes at the beginning of the summer. Dusshera and Durga Puja cover the same 10-day period, but Dusshera is linked to the legend of the god Ram, whereas Durga Puja is dedicated to the goddess Durga and is mainly celebrated in Bengal. Because most festivals were originally linked to harvest times, they happen at different times in north and south India, as the farming cycles are also different. Most of the major festivals in the south are linked to particular temples, like the great elephant parades seen in Kerala. Different regions have their own special festivals, but they are enjoyed by everyone.

LIGHT AND JOY
Lakshmi, the Hindu goddess of wealth and prosperity, is welcomed into homes at Diwali time. Everyone decorates their houses with little clay lamps called *diyas* and lots of candles. Firecrackers are set off to frighten off evil spirits.

Floating candle with rose petals

THE TEN-HEADED DEMON KING
Dusshera is the most important festival in North India. It lasts for 10 days, during which time everyone enjoys watching actors performing the story of Lord Ram and his wife Sita. On the final day, when Ram rescues Sita from Ravana, the evil demon-king of Lanka, huge effigies of Ravana are set ablaze in a burst of firecrackers.

CELEBRATING THE DIVINE
For Muslims, the death anniversaries of saints are important festival days. On these days, devotional songs called *qawwalis* are sung by professional singers in front of the saint's shrine (*dargah*). All festivals, especially those of Ramadan and Id, are also times of fasting or feasting.

Lead singer plays the harmonium, by squeezing the bellows

KUMBH MELA
A "*mela*" is a festival or fair, and the Kumbh Mela is one of the most important festivals for Hindus. Thousands upon thousands of devotees gather at the banks of the Ganges River in Allahabad to take a dip in the waters which are considered holy. Once every 144 years, the Maha (Great) Kumbh Mela takes place. Last time, in early 2001, more than 25 million pilgrims attended, making this the largest such gathering in the history of the world.

BATTLE OF THE TITANS

One of the most spectacular festivals in the whole country is called Puram. In April or May each year, the town of Thrissur, in Kerala, is filled with crowds who come to see a grand, and very noisy, display. There's a procession of 61 beautifully decorated elephants, from different temples. On top of the elephants are drummers, who enthusiastically compete to see who can drum fastest and loudest.

Mahouts (elephant drivers) balance long umbrellas on the elephant's head

Some festival candies are decorated with pure silver leaf

SWEET GREETINGS

A festival wouldn't be complete without candies (*mithais*). The shops are full of delicious candies, made from sugar and milk, and flavored with saffron, cardamoms, and rose water. People go from house to house distributing candies to friends and neighbors.

Swastika is a Hindu symbol

TIES OF AFFECTION

The festival of Raksha Bandhan celebrates the bond between brothers and sisters. Girls tie sacred threads (*rakhis*) on their brothers' wrists. In return, they receive gifts and the promise of everlasting protection and brotherly love.

RIOT OF COLOR

Children love the spring festival of Holi. As soon as the sun comes up, they rush around throwing colored powder at each other and squirting colored water from water pistols and pumps. Getting drenched and stained from head to foot is all part of the fun. Holi marks the end of winter and the first harvest of the new season.

Index

Acknowledgements

Dorling Kindersley would like to thank:
National Museum; Crafts Museum; Sanskriti; City Palace Museum, Jaipur. Monica Byles, Jane Tetzlaff and Bindia Thapar for their invaluable development work. Sheema Mookherjee for proofing the entire book, Ranjana Saklani for help with the index, Suresh Kumar for his cartographic inputs, and Arun P. for the endpapers.

Additional picture research: Sally Hamilton
Additional photography: Akhil Bakhshi
The publisher would like to thank the following for their kind permission to reproduce their photographs:
Picture credits
t=top; tl=top left; tr=top right; c=center; cl=center left; cr= center right; b=bottom; bl=bottom left; bc=bottom centrer; br=bottom; right; a=above; b=below.
AGP PHOTOBANK/Jitendra Singh: 62tr;

Aditya Arya: 10bl, 31b, 32b; Aditya Patankar: 36tr, 38tr, 39tc; Akhil Bakhshi: 17c, 32tr, 33cl, 44tr; Amar Talwar: 19tr, 29br, 30tl/c, 31tl/tc, 33t/b; Ashok Diwali: 7b; Amit Pasricha: 26cr, 48b; Avinash Pasricha: 46c/bl, 47br, 49bl/br; Ashmolean Museum: 59cr; Ronald Mackecitnie: 22tr; Bobby Kholi: 24br, 25b; Benoy K Behl: 12 -13b, 13br; Benu Joshi: 53b; B. P. S. Walia :26-27b, 47tr; Bimla Verma: 35cr, 38cr, 40br, 62tl; British Library: 42cl; British Museum, London: 10c, 12tl; Central London Gurudwara/Gary Ombler: 59tl/tlb; Clare Arni: 7tr, 32cr; CORBIS/Gianni Dagli: 24tr; Jeffrey L Rotman: 24c; DK PICTURE LIBRARY: 38br, 44cl, 47b, 57bl, 58tr/bl, Alex Wilson: 17crb, Alistair Duncan: 53trb, Aditya Patankar: 14br, 18c, 35tl, 37br, 43b, 54b, 61tl, 62cb; Amit Pasricha: 25tl, 29c, 32tl/cl, 33c, 52trb; Barnabas Kindersly: 10br, 63cr, Cyril

Laubscher: 52tl, David Murray: 17cb/bla, 57tcb/tcr, Dave King:14tr, 44-45b, David Exton: 57br/brb, Dinesh Khanna: 6tl, 20cl/bl, 20-21cb, 21tl/tr, 50bl, 51tr/bl/b, Fredrik Arvidsson: 17br, Harry Taylor: 41c, Ian O'Leary: 57tc, Jerry Young: 53br, M. Balan: 30bl/br, 41tc, 53bl, 56tr, Martin Norris: 50cl, Neil Fletcher: 57tr/c, Ram Rahman: 50tl, 59bl, Sanjay Sharma: 24tl, 33cr, 38bc, 40tl, 60b, 63cl, Steve Gorton: 53tr, 57tl, Subhash Bhargava: 51tr, Tim Ridley: 56tl,Toby Sinclair: 6br; Deepak Sanan: 37tl; Dinesh Khanna: 48tr-49tl; Fotomedia: 23tcb, 25tr, 38cl, 41tr, 43tr, 49tr; Glasgow Museum: 44tl, 58br, 59cl; Hulton Getty, London/Edward Gooch: 22-23b; India Picture/Unesco Parzor: 61tr; India Today Magazine: 55tr; John Frost Historical Newspapers: 27cr; Link Picture Library/Chandra Kishore Prasad: 26tl/tlb; M. Balan: 6bl, 63cr; Maryam Reshi: 37tr; National Railway Museum, New Delhi: 24bl; National Museum, New Delhi: 8tl/cl/bl/br, 9cl,12bl, 13tc/tca,18tl/tr, 19tl/br, 21br, 22tl, 41tl, 43tl, 46tl, 54c/cr,

55tl, 56b, R.C. Dutta Gupta: 9tl/c/ca/cr, 13tl/tlb, J. C. Arora: 13tr, 16bl, P. Roy: 41cl; National Gallery Of Modern Art, New Delhi/Akhil Bakhshi: 9b, 34c; Outlook Magazine: 28tl, 55c; Pallava Bagla: 29bl; Phal S. Girota: 30tr; Prem Kapoor: 12br, 29cr; Press Information Bureau: 29t; Pitt Rivers Museum:15tl; Powell Cotton Museum, London: 11tr; R. S. Chundawat: 52tr; Robin Wiginton/Arbour Antiques: 2tr; Roli Books: 15tr, 34bl; Rom Whitaker: 27tr; Rupinder Khullar: 40bl; Sanjay Sharma: 39bl, 48tl; Shalini Saran: 10tl, 11tl,15b, 20tl, 45br, 59br; Subhash Bhargava: 7tc, 31tr, 36bl, 39br, 42tr, 60bl; T. S. Satyan: 51br, 55bl; The Hindustan Times: 28b; Teen Murti Library, New Delhi: 28cr; Toby Sinclair: 7tl, 8c, 23tc/tr, 24bla, 53tl, 62-63bb; V. Muthuraman: 7cl, 16br, 35bl, 58tl, 61br; V. K. Rajamani: 22cl; Victoria and Albert Museum / Mike Kitcatt: 24c; Wallace Collection, London/Geoff Dann: 14bl/bc; Every effort has been made to trace the copyright holders of photographs. The publishers apologize for any omissions.